# MIKE PIAZZA

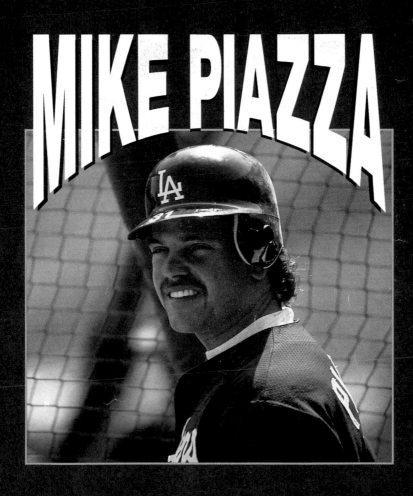

# MIKE PIAZZA
## Hard-Hitting Catcher

Jeff Savage

Lerner Publications Company • Minneapolis

Information for this book was obtained from the author's interviews with John "Doc" Kennedy, Dave Mitchell, Tony Nattle, Joe Pizzica, and the following sources: *Bill Mazeroski's Baseball Magazine, Gentleman's Quarterly,* Los Angeles Dodgers public relations department, *Los Angeles Times, New York Times, Orange County Register, San Francisco Chronicle, Sport, Sports Illustrated, The Sporting News, USA Today Baseball Weekly.*

*This book is available in two editions:*
Library binding by Lerner Publications Company
Soft cover by First Avenue Editions
241 First Avenue North, Minneapolis, Minnesota 55401

Copyright © 1997 by Jeff Savage

LIBRARY OF CONGRESS CATALOGING-IN-PUBLICATION DATA

**Savage, Jeff, 1961–**
  Mike Piazza, hard-hitting catcher / Jeff savage.
    p.   cm. — (The achievers)
  Includes bibliographical references (p.   ) and index.
  Summary: Describes the life and achievements of the Los Angeles Dodgers' star catcher and power-hitter who was voted National League Rookie of the Year in 1993.
  ISBN 0-8225-2895-9 (alk. paper). — ISBN 0-8225-9752-7 (pbk. : alk. paper)
  1. Piazza, Mike, 1968—  —Juvenile literature. 2. Baseball players— United States—Biography—Juvenile literature. 3. Los Angeles Dodgers (Baseball team)—Juvenile literature. [1. Piazza, Mike, 1968–   . 2. Baseball players.] I. Title. II. Series.
GV865.P52S32    1997
796.357'092
[B]—dc21                                                      96–54063

Manufactured in the United States of America
1  2  3  4  5  6  –  JR  –  02  01  00  99  98  97

# Contents

Mike smacks a home run during the 1996 All-Star Game.
He got more All-Star votes than any other player.

# An All-Star Night

From the dugout, Mike Piazza looked up at the children leaning over the metal railing. Holding pens and scorebooks, they were pleading for autographs from the players on the field. Not too long ago, Mike thought to himself, he had stood exactly where they were, hanging over that very same railing. Now he was a grown man and a baseball player, a catcher for the Los Angeles Dodgers, about to play in the 1996 All-Star Game. He had come back to Veterans Stadium in Philadelphia because the fans had asked him. All across the country, the fans asked him by marking his name on the All-Star ballot. Mike had gotten more votes than any other catcher in the National League. He had gotten more than any other player!

Mike looked away from the children at the railing and out to the field where a large man dressed in a coat and tie stood near the pitcher's mound. It was

Mike Schmidt. Schmidt had played third base for the Phillies a decade earlier. He is in the baseball Hall of Fame. Mike remembered himself as a boy, sitting with his father in the seats behind third base and watching the moves of his hero, Mike Schmidt.

"Piazza? You ready?" someone called out. Mike rose nervously, popped his catcher's mitt a few times with his fist, and ran up the dugout steps to the field. Schmidt was about to throw out the ceremonial first pitch. Mike had been asked to catch it.

Schmidt waved to the cheering crowd. Then he reared back and threw the baseball toward home plate. Mike caught the ball and squeezed hard. Schmidt walked up and shook Mike's hand. Then he took the ball from Mike's glove and showed it to him. There was an inscription on the ball that read: "To Mike Piazza. Wishing you the best. I think you're the best. Your friend, Mike Schmidt." Schmidt smiled at Mike and put the ball back in his glove. Mike squeezed it harder.

Vince Piazza was watching his son from the stands behind third base. He could hardly believe what was happening. Vince had owned these seats in section 122 since the day the stadium, nicknamed the Vet, had opened in 1971. Here he was, watching his son catch the opening pitch from the great Mike Schmidt. About 50 Piazza relatives and friends were seated around Mike's father.

Fans love to talk to Mike and get his autograph.

The only person missing was Tommy Lasorda. The Dodgers manager was supposed to be in the dugout, coaching the National League team. Instead, he was on his couch back home in Los Angeles. Two weeks earlier, Lasorda had suffered a heart attack. He wanted to be in Philadelphia to see Vince Piazza, his old friend, and to be with Mike, but the doctors had ordered Lasorda to stay home. They even told him not to watch the game on television because the stress might be too much for his heart. But Lasorda watched the game anyway.

Mike had telephoned his manager just that morning.

Manager Tommy Lasorda helped Mike get started.

Lasorda told his young catcher not to be nervous, to just go out and have fun. Mike tried to appear cool on the outside as he squatted down behind the plate to start the game. But inside, his stomach was doing flip-flops.

John Smoltz of the Braves, the starting pitcher for the National League, had been nearly perfect all year. Maybe Smoltz was nervous, too, because the first American League batter to face him, Kenny Lofton of the Indians, rapped a single to center. But Smoltz soon found his groove. First, he got Wade Boggs of the Yankees to pop up to the shortstop. Next, Roberto Alomar of the Orioles flied out to centerfield. Finally, powerful Albert Belle of the Indians missed three pitches for a strikeout. Mike hustled to the dugout to remove his catcher's gear. He was scheduled to be the fifth hitter.

San Francisco's Barry Bonds drove in the game's first run with a grounder to first. Mike stood, waiting, in the **on-deck circle** as Fred McGriff of the Braves batted. When McGriff struck out for the National League's third out, Mike rushed back to the dugout to put on his gear. He would have to wait until the second inning for his turn at bat.

Smoltz breezed through the American League batters in the next inning. Then Mike got his chance. The television camera showed him step into the batter's box in his Los Angeles Dodger uniform. Mike is 6-foot-3 and weighs about 215 pounds. He has a soft face with big brown eyes and rosy cheeks. Power hitters aren't supposed to look nice, though, so Mike wore a mustache that fanged downward to his chin. The mustache made Mike look scary. His massive Popeye-like arms would frighten any pitcher. Mike held the bat high and cocked forward as he waited for Charles Nagy's first pitch. "Ball one!" cried the umpire.

The next pitch was a fastball headed for the inside corner. Mike leaned into it, swung, and fouled it

11

back. That wasn't his pitch. He likes to hit the ball when it is farther out over the plate. Mike knew he had to be patient.

The next pitch came in too high. "Ball two!" said the umpire. Mike chewed softly on the single stick of gum in his mouth and stared out at the pitcher. The outfielders were positioned fairly deep. They knew what Mike could do. Nagy whirled and threw the ball. In an instant, Mike decided it was the pitch he wanted. He strode forward with his front foot, straightened up on his front leg, and swept his mighty arms around. Boom! Mike got a good, full smack with the barrel of his bat and sent the ball screaming to left. His bat whipped clear around his body and struck him across the letter P on the back of his uniform. Television announcer Bob Costas yelled, "Good-bye! Absolutely crushed!"

Nagy's head spun around to watch the ball. American League fielders Wade Boggs at third base and Cal Ripken Jr. at shortstop turned together and watched it go. The ball sailed high into the Philadelphia night. Leftfielder Albert Belle didn't even move. He knew it was a homer when the ball left the bat. A rush went through Mike. He dropped his bat at the plate and started his trot around the bases. The ball didn't land in the seats until after Mike had touched first base and was on his way to second. The ball landed in the upper deck of the stands.

Mike trots home after his booming hit at the All-Star Game.

Mike's National League teammates congratulate him.

Back in Los Angeles, Tommy Lasorda jumped off his couch. He screamed, "It's gone! It's out of here!" Lasorda's wife, Jo, yelled, "Take it easy! Take it easy!" but Lasorda jumped around the room.

When Mike circled the bases, he wasn't running as much as he was floating. When he hit third and turned for home, he could almost hear the shouts of his father and the people in section 122. Mike stepped on home plate and Dante Bichette of the Rockies gave him a high five. Chipper Jones of the Braves shook Mike's hand by the on-deck circle. Mike stepped down into the dugout with a big smile. Barry Bonds was the first to greet him. Then all the other players were shaking Mike's hand and patting him on the helmet.

The home run was measured at 445 feet. Only two or three shots a year go that far at the Vet. The homer was even more amazing because Mike isn't a **pull hitter**. Most of his hits are to the **opposite field**, like the double he hit in the next inning.

Moments after Gary Sheffield of the Marlins caught the final out in rightfield for the National League's 6–0 victory, the Most Valuable Player award ceremony was held near home plate. Mike Piazza was the winner. "I'm very honored and I'm really choked up," Mike said as he held the heavy silver MVP trophy.

Photographers and reporters followed Mike up the stadium tunnel toward the clubhouse where his father was waiting. Vince put his arms around his son and squeezed him. Then Mike disappeared through the clubhouse doors. "It's a dream fulfilled," Vince said. "What else is left? It's a dream come true. I keep pinching myself to make sure that this is real."

Back in Los Angeles, Tommy Lasorda was back on his couch when his phone rang. "Michael has made me very, very proud of him," Lasorda told the reporter who called. "What a show he put on tonight. What a great, great story."

In Philadelphia, Mike answered reporters' questions after the game. "I never imagined doing anything heroic or out of a storybook," he told them. "I just didn't want to look bad. I was just hoping I didn't embarrass myself in my hometown."

An All-Star when he was a 15-year-old, Mike played for the Phoenixville team in the Babe Ruth league.

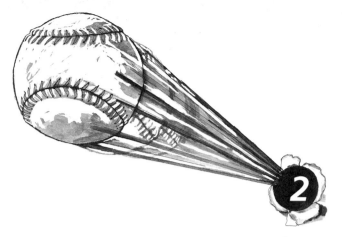

# *In the Cage*

The house on Spring Lane where Mike lived as a boy was ordinary for the town of Phoenixville. It was dark green, had two stories, and was just big enough to hold Mike's parents, Vince and Veronica Piazza, Mike's brothers, Vince Jr., Danny, Tony, and Tommy, and Mike. Mike's room was ordinary, too. It had a bed and a nightstand and a dresser for his clothes, and its walls were covered with pennants and posters and pictures of his favorite baseball players. Mike was born September 4, 1968, and even his earliest memories are of baseball.

Vince Piazza was the grandson of a mill worker who came to America from Italy. Vince sold land and used cars. Later, he bought a computer company. Eventually, Vince became wealthy and moved his family to a bigger house. But for the first 13 years of Mike's life, before his father got rich, he lived in that ordinary house on Spring Lane. What was behind the house wasn't so ordinary. Behind the house was the cage.

The cage was a large enclosed structure made of wood paneling and planks and nails, along with a large net. Mike's father had built it with some spare lumber.

At one end of the cage was an automatic pitching machine. Mike would load the machine with about 20 battered baseballs. Then he would run with his aluminum bat to the other end of the cage and get into position. The machine would make a whirring sound and then shoot a ball toward him every 10 seconds or so with a loud thump. Mike would step out of his crouch and swing hard at the ball. If he hit it properly, which he usually did, it would make a resounding ping and sail past the machine and hit the net with a spish. That was the sound always coming from behind the dark green house on Spring Lane. Thump. Ping. Spish. . . . Thump. Ping. Spish.

In the winter, Mike would shovel the snow in the cage until he had enough room to take a full swing. He would heat the baseballs on the kitchen stove, and he would wrap insulation around the bat handle or wear mittens so his hands wouldn't sting.

"The guy practically lived in that batting cage," said his friend Joe Pizzica. "Day or night. Summer or winter. Every time I called him, his mother would answer and say the same thing: 'He's out in the cage, Joe.'"

Mike's hitting in high school baseball impressed fans.

When Mike wasn't in the cage, he was usually down at the dam in Pickering Creek. Pickering Creek flows into the Schuylkill River, which runs south to Philadelphia where it empties into the Delaware River. At the dam, where the creek is widest, a big tree stood at the edge of the bank. A rope hung from the tree. Mike and his friends would take turns swinging from the rope into the creek.

More than anything, though, Mike loved baseball. Mike's father and Dodgers manager Tommy Lasorda were close childhood friends who grew up in nearby Norristown, Pennsylvania. Whenever the Dodgers came to town to play the Phillies, Mike would go into the clubhouse with his father. When Mike was nine, the Dodgers clinched the National League pennant in Philadelphia. Mike watched in wonder as grown men went running around the clubhouse in their under-wear, celebrating and dumping champagne on one an-other. "To me," Mike says, "it was 'Wow, that's what I want to do. I want to win a World Series. I want to be the champion.'"

That same year, Mike joined his first Little League team—the A's. His coach, Abdul Ford-Bey, taught him that the game is as hard as the baseball. Mike and his teammates learned as much about discipline as they did about fundamentals. They ran wind sprints and did lots of fingertip push-ups.

Mike joined the Cardinals the following year, and that coach made him play catcher. "Mike wasn't too fond of the position," said his friend Tony Nattle. "He didn't like putting on the equipment, and the heat was draining on him. He had no intention of being a catcher ever again."

What Mike wanted to be, when he wasn't standing in the batter's box, was a pitcher. Mike developed a strong arm and learned to throw a **curveball.** When Mike was 13, he led the Phoenixville All-Stars to the district title. He pitched the semifinal game and hit the winning home run. In the final, he started the game playing first base. When the Phoenixville starting pitcher ran into trouble, Mike came in to pitch. Phoenixville was leading 8–6 when Mike took the mound. With two outs and the bases loaded in the seventh, Mike's friend Joe Pizzica came over from third base.

"Listen," Mike said, "if we get this last guy out right here, we make the state playoffs." "How do you want to play it?" asked Joe. "I've got an idea," Mike said. "Let's get him out together, you and me."

Mike delivered the first pitch high and tight. The batter swung and popped the ball up to third base. Pizzica caught it for the final out. Mike was mobbed at the mound by his teammates. Pizzica stood staring at the ball in his glove. "That's when I knew about Mike," he said. "I knew he could be as good as he wanted."

Mike was in the cage one day when his father told him some good news. Mike could be a batboy for the Dodgers whenever they came to Philadelphia. Mike already knew Tommy Lasorda, but this meant Mike would get to meet the players.

Mike's friends noticed a change in him the next day. Mike was normally a quiet student, but in Mr. Uliano's ninth-grade Spanish class, he was suddenly sitting up on the edge of his chair and asking questions. Each day, Mike would ask his teacher about certain words and phrases. His friends soon found out that the Dodgers had a sensational rookie pitcher named Fernando Valenzuela. Valenzuela was from Mexico. He spoke Spanish, and Mike wanted to be able to talk with him.

As a batboy, Mike's duties were simple. He shagged baseballs that strayed near the visitor's dugout, he retrieved the bat at home plate used by the Dodger batter and returned it to the bat rack, and sometimes he provided the umpire with a handful of baseballs. Mike was thrilled to be in the dugout with the players. He loved to walk onto the field, surrounded by thousands of fans and dressed in his blue Dodger uniform with his name stitched across the back. He got to know the players' hitting styles by watching them take batting practice in the cage before the game. He was especially awed by the swings of Steve Garvey, Ron Cey, Dusty Baker, and Pedro Guerrero. Coach Lasorda would often say, half-kiddingly, to Mike's father that maybe someday Mike would be wearing Dodger blue for real. When Mike heard this, he blushed but he never turned away. He took the idea seriously.

Mike is the fourth from the left in the back row.

Around this time, the Piazza family packed its belongings and moved four miles east. The Piazzas had bought a stretch of land on Valley Forge Mountain. An enormous house was in the middle of the land. The house had a wraparound cobblestone driveway in front and a golf course on one side. From the view out back, Mike could see the National Historic Park in which George Washington's troops had slept during the American Revolutionary War.

A batting cage was built for Mike in the basement of the house. The basement was at ground level. Mike could look out over the stables and the whole valley. He could even see the barn in which Washington had slept. But Mike cared more about seeing the curveball from the pitching machine.

Mike could program his machine to deliver different pitches. He practiced against an assortment of fastballs, curveballs, and even **knuckleballs.** Mike had big boxes filled with major league baseballs that he got for being a batboy. Sometimes, he would hit these balls in the cage.

Mike developed other interests as well. He listened to rock music, and he had an electric guitar and a big amplifier that he sometimes played in his room. Mike also began to play the drums. He hung out at the arcade with his friends at the King of Prussia mall. He played on the golf team in high school, but he wasn't so good at golf. One time, he and Joe Pizzica were hitting golf balls from Joe's front lawn when Mike sliced one over some houses. The next thing they heard was a crash. The boys ran and hid behind a bush until they figured the coast was clear. They were walking down the street to see what damage they had done when they noticed a man coming up the sidewalk toward them. He was bouncing a golf ball. The man walked right by them. Frozen with terror, they watched him go straight to Joe's house and knock on the front door. They turned and ran farther down the street, cut between some houses, and circled around until they ended up in Joe's backyard. They sneaked alongside the house and stopped when they saw the man on the driveway talking with Joe's parents. Their hearts pounded with fear. They stood there for what seemed like an hour. Finally the man left. They came out from hiding and got into plenty of trouble.

As much as Mike enjoyed being with his friends, he always put baseball first. "Mike always was the first to leave a party," his friend Dave Mitchell says. "He knew exactly what he was doing. We thought maybe his parents told him he had to be home early. But really, we knew that wasn't it. We knew it was him. He had a plan. He wanted to go home. He wanted to get in that cage."

Throughout his time at Phoenixville High School, Mike kept his focus on playing professional baseball.

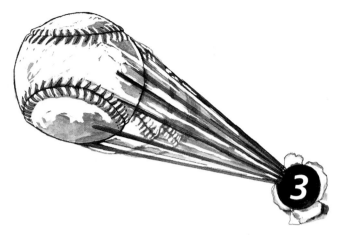

# High School Slugger

The Phoenixville High Phantoms needed a catcher. John "Doc" Kennedy, coach of the Phantoms, knew Mike would try out for the team. Kennedy remembered Mike from Little League. He knew that Mike had a strong arm, perfect for throwing out base runners. Plus, Mike didn't run so fast. Of all the positions, a catcher has to run the least.

A few weeks before the season began, coach Kennedy approached Mike in the library. "Hey, Michael," the coach said, "I have an important question to ask you. Have you ever considered being a catcher?"

Mike was surprised at the question. "A catcher?" Mike didn't know what to say. He hated playing catcher, but he didn't want to upset his new coach. "I don't know," he finally said. "Can I think about it?"

Mike didn't mind the idea of not pitching anymore.

He wanted to concentrate on his hitting. But he figured he would play first base, as he had for the Phoenixville Junior High Blue Hawks, or any position but catcher.

At school the next day, coach Kennedy asked Mike if he had thought about catching. "Yeah, Coach, I thought about it," Mike said. "If it's all right with you, I'd rather stay at first base."

Coach Kennedy accepted Mike's decision. The coach wouldn't make someone play a position they didn't want to play. But the varsity team already had a senior to play first base. So Mike spent 10th grade with the junior varsity.

The junior varsity and varsity teams traveled together on the bus for road games, and Mike enjoyed hanging out with the older players. That is, until the trip to Pottsgrove. Some seniors sitting in the back of the bus were spitting chewing tobacco juice into little white cups. They acted as if they enjoyed it. Mike had never tried tobacco. He thought this would be a good time to start.

The seniors waved him back and Mike sat down among them. One of the seniors produced a thin, round canister with a tin lid. He pulled the lid back to reveal a clump of brownish powder. "Take a big pinch," he said. "Stick it behind your lip." Mike put the tobacco in his mouth.

Mike grinned and sat there with a mouthful of tobacco as everyone watched him. At first, Mike didn't mind the taste so much. But with each passing moment, the taste got worse and worse. Soon Mike's grin turned to a grimace. The flavor was bitter and rotten as it passed down his tongue and up into the roof of his mouth. What a disgusting taste!

Mike tried to spit the tobacco on the floor but it was all mixed around in his mouth. He swallowed and nearly gagged. Suddenly, Mike felt as if his throat were on fire! His face went hot, and he began shaking and gasping for air. It was pure torture! The seniors laughed. "You should have seen him," his friend Dave Mitchell remembers. "His face turned purple and then all different colors."

Mike got so sick he couldn't play in the game that day. He sat alone in the dugout with his head in his hands and that foul taste still in his mouth. He never tried tobacco again.

Mike joined the varsity as a junior, and his baseball life blossomed. Against defending champion Boyertown High in the second game of the season, the Phantoms had two runners on with two outs in the first inning when Mike came up. He smacked the first pitch he saw deep to right-centerfield. The ball sailed over the chain-link fence and landed on City Line Avenue nearly 400 feet away. It was a terrific blast, and Mike raced around the bases for his first varsity home run.

Teammates come out to cheer another Piazza homer.

Two days later, the Phantoms played at Owen J. Roberts High. The first four batters singled to give the Phantoms a 2–0 lead. Then it was Mike's turn. He let two balls pass by, then crushed the third pitch to dead centerfield. It soared high and far and cleared the fence easily. The Phoenixville players mobbed Mike at home plate. They were thrilled to have such a great power hitter. In the fifth inning, Mike did it again. With a runner on first, he turned on a pitch and lifted it high down the leftfield line. The ball sailed over the fence and Mike circled the bases for his second blast of the game.

Mike hit a homer in his fifth game and another in his sixth. By Phoenixville's 10th game, Mike was leading the team in every hitting category. Coach Kennedy moved him up to the **cleanup spot.** Mike homered and doubled in that game, too.

After another homer and double at Pottstown High, a story about Mike appeared in the *Pottstown Mercury.* Mike told the reporter that Dodgers batting coach Manny Mota had given him some hitting tips. "Manny noticed that I was **uppercutting** a little too much, which is what a power hitter often does," Mike told the newspaper. "Manny told me to keep my head down and try to swing down on the ball."

In the last five games of the season, Mike hit five more home runs. He finished the year with 12, breaking the school record set two decades earlier by Andre Thornton. Thornton had gone on to become a star player for the Cleveland Indians. Mike was an easy choice as the team's Most Valuable Player.

One Saturday morning in the summer, a visitor came to the Piazza house for breakfast. It was Ted Williams, one of the greatest sluggers ever. Williams had played for the Boston Red Sox from 1939 to 1960. In 1941, Williams had a **batting average** of .406. No major league hitter since 1941 has hit above .400 for an entire season. Williams also hit 521 home runs in his career. Mike's father had met Williams, a Hall of Famer, through a friend.

"I couldn't even talk because I was so nervous," Mike remembered. After breakfast, Williams went with Mike to the basement cage to watch him hit. The family recorded the event on videotape. The pitching machine whirred. Thump. Ping. Spish. . . . Mike blasted the balls with everything he had. "Mike hits the ball harder than I did when I was 16," Williams said to the video camera. "I guarantee you, this kid will hit the ball. I never saw anybody who looked better at his age." When Williams asked Mike, "Son, do you have my book on hitting?" Mike nodded and smiled. He had memorized Williams's book.

In his senior year, Mike homered in his first **at bat,** and he never stopped. At Great Valley High in his second game, he struck out his first time up. The next inning, Mike belted a **grand slam.** He got three hits in three at bats in the third game with three **runs batted in (RBIs).** He hit a home run in each of his next four games.

Ted Williams played for the Boston Red Sox. He was one of the best hitters in the history of the game.

Mike still worked as a batboy when the Dodgers came to Veterans Stadium. Coach Lasorda let Mike take batting practice with the players. Veteran Alejandro Pena was pitching one day when Mike lashed a bullet past Pena's ear. The hit landed on the warning track. Pena threw the next pitch under Mike's chin. The message: baseball isn't as easy as you think.

When Mike went back to the Phantoms, no pitcher seemed able to stop him. Mike homered at Unionville High, he homered at Coatesville, and he homered at Spring Ford. He was batting nearly .600.

Mike slides into third, hoping to avoid a tag.

Mike clinched the Chest-Mont League title for his team on a beautiful spring day in May. Batting against rival Downington, Mike hit two home runs in the game—a leadoff shot to rightfield in the third that reached City Line Avenue and a two-run bomb to leftfield in the fourth that carried clear to the football practice field. He scored three times and drove in six runs in the game—after striking out in the first inning!

Phoenixville's season ended with a 3–2 loss in the district semifinals. The baseball careers of most high school players end at this point.

Mike knew that his parents wanted him to go to college, but he was hoping to join the Dodgers. Each June, officials from each of the major league baseball teams get together for the baseball draft. They take turns choosing players who have graduated from high school or who are playing in college. The officials offer the players money to play baseball for their teams. Usually the players are sent to minor league teams to improve before they play with the major league teams.

The Dodgers never called Mike. Neither did any other major league team. The baseball draft ended with Mike still sitting by his telephone.

Mike didn't realize that hundreds of slow-footed power-hitting first basemen graduate from high school every year. All he knew was he had to get to the big leagues somehow. Mike enrolled at the University of Miami, which has an excellent baseball program. He figured he could impress the pro scouts by playing top-notch college ball. But Miami has so many skilled athletes that freshmen rarely get to play. In his first year, Mike mostly sat at the end of the bench. He got nine at bats all year. He got one hit.

Mike was desperate. Time was slipping away. He didn't want to sit on the bench. He wanted to play. He transferred to nearby Miami-Dade North Community College where he got to play every game.

Out in Los Angeles, Dodgers manager Lasorda was badgering scouting director Ben Wade to send a scout to Florida to check out Mike. Wade finally sent a scout named Bill Pleis. Mike was hitting .364 for the season, but on the day Pleis watched him play, Mike didn't get a hit. Pleis returned to Los Angeles. On Mike's scouting report, Pleis wrote, "Forget it."

Lasorda didn't give up. In June, he begged Wade to draft Mike anyway. "Put him on the bottom of the list," Lasorda pleaded. "Make him the last guy." That's how Mike was drafted by the Dodgers in the 62nd round of the 1988 draft. The 62nd round was the last round. Mike was the 1,389th player chosen.

Mike received the news in a letter. The Dodger scouts didn't really think he was good enough to join their organization. They didn't bother to call him until two months later. When they did, Mike begged them for a tryout.

A week later, Mike was standing in the batter's box at Dodger Stadium, staring out at a batting practice pitcher. Coach Lasorda and scouting director Wade were seated in the stands. This was Mike's tryout. This was his big chance and Mike made the most of it. "I just hammered balls," he said.

While attending Miami-Dade North Community College, Mike was drafted by the Dodgers.

Lasorda turned to Wade and asked, "If he was a catcher who could hit balls into the seats like that, would you sign him?" Wade said he would. "Then he's a catcher," Lasorda said. Wade disagreed. He pointed out that Mike had been playing first base.

As Mike continued to blast home runs, Wade gave in. "O.K., O.K.," he said. "Let me see him throw." Mike threw as hard as he could. Wade agreed to sign Mike to a contract. He offered Mike $15,000. "I said yes before he said 'thousand,'" Mike said. "He could have said $15 and it wouldn't have mattered."

Wade called Bill Pleis and said, "Listen, Bill, don't get upset, but I'm going to sign this kid. He hit 'em where I'd never seen 'em hit before . . . and he says he'll catch."

Being drafted, even in the last round, made Mike smile.

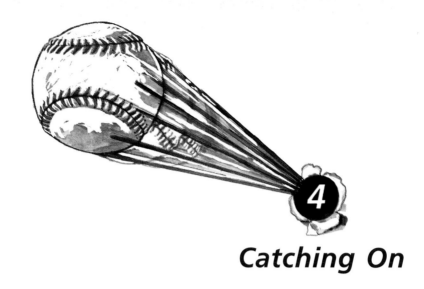

# Catching On

Catcher. That dreadful position was suddenly Mike's ticket to the big leagues. Mike didn't know much about being a catcher, but he knew he had better learn—fast.

Major league teams develop young players in their "farm systems." A farm system is an organization of minor league teams at different levels. The first level is a rookie league, which is for players who have just signed a contract. The next level is Class A, then Class AA, and, finally, Class AAA. The level after Class AAA is the major leagues.

In March, Mike arrived at the Dodgers' spring training facility in Vero Beach, Florida. The Dodgers have a huge complex with six baseball fields, outdoor and indoor batting cages, apartments for coaches and players to live in, and a large stadium. Many people consider the Dodgers' spring training site to be the best spring training facility in baseball. Since it's nearly as big as a town, it is called Dodgertown. Each spring, all the Dodgers, from the big-leaguers down to the rookie-leaguers, come to Dodgertown. Mike was thrilled to be a rookie-leaguer at Dodgertown.

Instructor John Roseboro, a retired Dodgers catcher, was assigned to help Mike. Roseboro started at the beginning. He taught Mike how to put on the catcher's gear. Next, he taught Mike how to squat behind the plate. Then he taught the rookie how to hold the catcher's mitt and how to relay signs from the dugout to the pitcher.

Eventually, Mike was assigned to a team in Salem, Oregon, in the rookie Northwest League. When Mike arrived, he discovered that the Salem field was nothing more than an old sandlot. Players had to pick rocks out of the infield and sweep it with brooms. The dugout was a weather-beaten old shack. The wobbly chain-link fence in the outfield looked as if it could collapse at any moment.

The visiting fields weren't in much better shape, and players rode a bus to their away games. Mike was responsible for his baseball uniform and his equipment—his bats and catcher's gear. The team gave him $11 a day for meals. Most games were played at night, so Mike usually didn't eat dinner until after midnight. Then he often ate at fast-food restaurants, such as Denny's, Taco Bell, or Domino's Pizza.

Mike heard some players whisper that he was Tommy Lasorda's pet. Such talk bothered him, but he didn't say anything. He just concentrated on learning to catch. Mike finished the season with a solid .288 batting average, 8 home runs, and 25 RBIs. He hit 6 homers in one week during a spurt like he hadn't had since he played for Phoenixville High. In one game against the A's at Medford, the Dodgers were losing 8–0 when Mike hit a three-run home run to cut the lead. The Dodgers chipped away to make it 8-6. Then, in the ninth inning, Mike hit another three-run homer to win the game.

The season ended in August. The players went home to rest and relax until the next spring. Everyone went home, that is, except Mike. He asked the Dodgers to send him to Campo Las Palmas, the Dodgers' baseball school in the Dominican Republic. No American had ever enrolled there. Mike became the first. "I knew I had a tremendous amount of work to do [to learn to play catcher]," he said.

Mike lived for three months in a dormitory with 40 other players who spoke only Spanish. He found tarantulas in his bunk bed. He ate beans and rice and drank sugarcane juice every day. But when Mike returned to the United States, he was a better catcher.

Mike joined the Class A Vero Beach team in 1990. By now, the rumor that Mike was Lasorda's pet was no longer kept to a whisper. Some of the players talked about it right in front of Mike. Mike even left the team once, prepared to quit baseball forever. Lasorda called him and talked him out of quitting. "People are always critical about something," Lasorda told Mike.

The next spring, legendary Dodgers catcher Roy Campanella helped Mike at Dodgertown. A Hall of Famer, Campanella gave Mike some good advice. "If you're always so concerned about the doors in life that are closing on you," Campanella said, "you're never going to see the ones that are opening."

Mike joined the Class A Bakersfield team in April with a fresh outlook. Bakersfield coach Tom Beyers, who had coached Mike two years earlier at Salem, noticed a big difference in the young catcher.

"I could see right away that he was much stronger," Beyers said. "I shook his hand and he just about crushed it. Later I saw why. He spent every chance he could squeezing those hand grips that strengthen your wrists and forearms. Except he didn't use those plastic grips. He used steel grips. Mike was doing everything he could to turn himself into a baseball player."

In Mike's first game, he showed what kind of season it was going to be by whacking a mammoth home run to centerfield. "You could see how much he had worked on his hitting," coach Beyers said. "He had learned to use his lower body, his hips, to generate more bat speed and create a more compact swing."

Former Dodger catcher Roy Campanella, center, coached Mike in how to catch. Campanella encouraged Mike.

Before long, Mike was the most feared hitter in the California League. One day late in the season, a pitcher decided to fight back. Mike had been hammering the High Desert Padres in a four-game series, drilling three **extra-base hits** in each of the first two games, and following up with a towering home run in the third game. The first time Mike was up after the home run, he dug in the batter's box. The pitcher looked in for the sign, nodded to the catcher, wound up and threw a fastball right at Mike's head.

Mike had to work his way up the ladder in the Dodgers' minor league system. Before reporting to the Class A Vero Beach team in the spring of 1990, Mike stopped at his parents' home to visit his family.

The ball hit Mike right on the temple. He crumpled to the ground and lay dazed for a moment. "He's lucky he didn't get killed," coach Beyers said. Somehow, Mike managed to get to his feet and walk to first base. He refused to leave the game. In his next at bat, Mike faced Tim Worrell. The coaches thought Mike would be afraid at the plate. Most hitters are after they get hit by a pitch. But Mike didn't act scared. He smacked the first pitch for a double off the wall. Coach Beyers leaned over to pitching coach Glen Gregson and whispered in amazement, "It didn't even faze him."

Mike posted huge numbers at Bakersfield. He batted .277 with 27 doubles, 29 home runs, 80 RBIs, and a **slugging percentage** of .540. He topped all Class A players in the country in extra-base hits.

Mike continued to pound the ball at every level. He started the 1992 season on the Class AA San Antonio team. He batted .322 with seven homers and 20 RBIs. In June, he was promoted to the Class AAA Albuquerque team, just one step from the big leagues. There, he led all Pacific Coast League catchers with a team-high .341 average, 16 homers, and 69 RBIs. In late August, Mike got the announcement he had been working for so hard. He was being called up to the big club. Just as Tommy Lasorda had jokingly predicted, Mike would get to wear Dodger blue for real.

Mike joined the Dodgers on September 1 in Chicago. It was a hot summer day. Above the ivy-covered walls and the bleachers, the sky was a scorching blue. Mike glanced at the lineup card in the dugout. He was stunned to see his name penciled in as the starting catcher. Mike Scioscia was the team's regular catcher, but the Dodgers were on their way to their worst record since 1905. The coaches wanted to see how Mike would do.

Mike's first major league at bat came in the second inning, with two outs and no one on base. He faced hard-throwing Mike Harkey. Mike knew he had to keep cool. He couldn't just flail away at anything. The Dodgers might send him right back to the minors. Mike was so excited he could hardly bear it, but he surprised even himself with his patience. He worked Harkey for a walk. The next batter popped out, but Mike had hung in there and gotten on base.

Mike next came up in the fourth inning. When Harkey delivered ball one, Mike began to wonder if he ever would take a swing. He did, on the next pitch. He cracked it clear to the ivy in right centerfield for a double! Mike hustled to second base and looked to the Dodger dugout. There, Tommy Lasorda was jumping up and down.

Mike came through again in the sixth. He drilled one of Harkey's fastballs for a single. In the eighth, he laced a single to leftfield off Paul Assenmacher.

The Dodgers scored a run in the 13th inning to win 5–4. Mike finished the game with three hits in three at bats. He had proved that he belonged.

Mike's first big league home run came a week later at Dodger Stadium against the San Francisco Giants. With Lenny Webster on third and Eric Karros on second, Mike socked a pitch from Steve Reed over the rightfield fence. The Dodgers won, 7–0.

But Mike didn't do everything right. In a game at San Diego, the Dodgers and Padres were locked in a 1–1 tie. Jerald Clark of the Padres was at third base. Mike went to the mound to talk to pitcher Orel Hershiser, but he forgot to ask the umpire for a time-out. Clark raced in from third to steal home for the winning run. Mike was humiliated. "It was a very embarrassing moment," he told reporters. More blunders like that, Mike thought, and the Dodgers would never keep him.

His warm smile and friendly manner have made Mike a favorite of fans across the country.

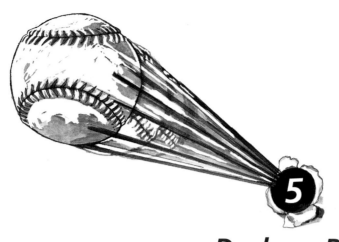

# *Dodger Blue*

When Mike arrived at Dodgertown the following spring, he received great news. The team had released Mike Scioscia. The starting catcher position was open.

Then the whispers started again. People said that Mike would get the job because he was a friend of Lasorda's. A rumor spread that Mike was Lasorda's godson. (Mike's youngest brother, Tommy Jr., is the manager's godson.) "I can remember 99 interviews that began 'Tell me about this godfather thing,'" Mike said. "One time I heard some guy ask Tommy 'If Piazza gets the job, it'll be because he earns it and not because of your relationship, right?' And this was right in front of me. It was uncomfortable."

Roy Campanella noticed that the whispers were bothering Mike. Campanella decided to give the young player another piece of advice. "Michael," he said, "you're going to be reading a lot of things in the paper, people are going to be talking about you, other players are going to talk about you. The most important thing is to go out and play."

So that is what Mike did. He hit .478 in the spring and socked four homers. Coach Lasorda made a bold prediction. "Michael will be a marquee player for us, an impact player," the coach said. "People will come from all over the country to see him play."

Mike won the starting catcher's job. Right away, he showed he deserved it. In the second week of the season, Mike threw out seven straight base stealers, including six Cardinals. His hitting was even better. After three months, he was batting .331 with 15 home runs and 52 runs batted in.

On June 15 at Colorado, Mike had his first two-homer game. He hit a solo shot in the sixth inning and a two-run bomb in the eighth. Pitchers around the league were becoming concerned about the Dodgers' hot hitter.

Mike became friends with first baseman Eric Karros, and they shared a Manhattan Beach townhouse. Karros had been the National League Rookie of the Year the previous season. Maybe this year would be Mike's turn.

Mike was shocked and happy when he was named to the All-Star team. Mike struck out in his only at bat, but he was proud just to be there.

With practice, Mike became a strong defensive catcher.

Mike's mother, Veronica, and brother Dan attended the Rookie of the Year banquet for Mike.

By September, the long season had taken its toll. Mike was getting worn out. But he withstood the strain. In his last 15 games, he got 22 hits in 47 at bats, with 5 homers. On the last day, he eliminated the rival Giants from the playoffs with 2 home runs and 5 RBIs. For the season, Mike hit .318 with 35 home runs and 112 RBIs. As a catcher, he set a Dodgers record by throwing out 58 runners attempting to steal. Mike was a unanimous choice as Rookie of the Year.

He returned to Dodgertown in the spring of 1994, relaxed and confident. A month earlier, he had signed a three-year contract for $4.2 million—the largest guaranteed deal for a second-year player. Mike bought a $15,000 stereo sound system and put the rest of the cash in the bank. And then he started bashing the ball again.

In the first week of the season, Mike hit a monstrous 458-foot homer off Tom Glavine to beat the Braves at Dodger Stadium. Later that month, Mike blasted a three-run bomb to win a game at Shea Stadium in New York. In June, he clubbed a 477-foot grand slam off Mark Gardner in the second inning at Florida. Mike came back with another grand slam two weeks later against Colorado. Then he homered in four straight games. He made the All-Star team again and the Dodgers were in first place when disaster hit. The strike!

Baseball team owners and players could not agree on how much money the players should make. The players refused to play until an agreement was reached. On August 11, the owners canceled the rest of the season. The playoffs were canceled. The World Series was canceled.

Mike went back home to Valley Forge and took out his frustration in the cage. He hit for hours every day until his hands were sore. Even on New Year's Eve, while his friends were out celebrating, Mike was down in the basement, sweating like mad, socking pitch after pitch.

The owners and players haggled over a deal and finally reached an agreement. The 1995 season started —two weeks late. When it did, Mike was ready. He got two hits on opening day and just kept hitting. In a game at San Diego in early May, Mike walloped a shot that smacked off the rightfield wall. But as Mike rounded first, he slipped and fell. He landed hard on his thumb. Right away, he knew it was broken. Doctors put the thumb in a cast, and Mike was forced to sit on the bench. The pain was bad, but sitting was even worse.

At last, after three long weeks, the cast was removed. The doctors advised Mike to wait one more week to rest his thumb. But Mike was too antsy to wait any longer. He felt that he had rested enough. Mike begged manager Lasorda to let him play right away and Lasorda gave in. It was a good decision. In Mike's first game back, against the New York Mets, he cracked a two-run homer off Pete Harnisch to win the game.

Mike made the All-Star team again, and this game was extra special. Dodgers pitcher Hideo Nomo, a rookie from Japan, would be pitching. Nomo was nicknamed "The Tornado" because of his spinning windup. Together, he and Mike were taking the National League West Division by storm. Mike capped off a glorious night by hitting a game-tying home run off Texas pitcher Kenny Rogers.

Mike and Hideo Nomo were a winning pair for Los Angeles.

Mike's steady play behind the plate led the Dodgers to the 1995 National League West Division title.

Then, on a humid night in late August, Mike had his greatest game ever. He was playing at Veterans Stadium in Philadelphia, his childhood park. After drawing a walk in the first against the Phillies, Mike ripped a double down the line in the third to give his team a 1–0 lead. In the fifth inning, he doubled again. In the sixth, Chad Fonville was on third, Brett Butler on second, and Jose Offerman on first when Mike stepped into the batter's box. Mike socked a long homer to left for a grand slam. In his last at bat in the eighth, he smacked another homer, this one a two-run shot to right. He finished the night with two doubles, two homers, and seven RBIs. He also took over the lead in the batting race ahead of Tony Gwynn. Only two catchers have ever won the batting crown in the twentieth century—Bubbles Hargrave in 1926 and Ernie Lombardi in 1942.

In the final month of the 1995 season, Gwynn surged past Mike to win his fifth batting title. But Mike's .346 average was still impressive, and his .384 average on the road led all major leaguers. Mike's team finished first in something more important, too—the division race. The Dodgers clinched the title on the next-to-last day when Mike hit a two-run homer against the Padres.

In the first game of the playoffs against the Cincinnati Reds, Mike blasted a homer off Pete Schourek. But the Reds won the game, 7–2. Cincinnati then won the next two to sweep the Dodgers.

Still, Mike had proved he was the best player on the Dodgers. His three-year totals of 91 homers, 297 runs batted in, and .327 average was the best start for any catcher in history. Not even Johnny Bench, the best-hitting catcher ever, put up such numbers. In fact, nobody but Babe Ruth and Ted Williams had hit as many home runs and batted for a higher batting average than Mike in their first three years of play.

Suddenly, everybody wanted to be with Mike. He played golf with basketball star Charles Barkley. He hung out with wide receiver Raghib "Rocket" Ismail. He practiced his electric guitar and drums, and talked to some of his favorite heavy metal groups about singing with them. He made guest appearances on the television shows *Baywatch*, *Married . . . With Children*, and *The Bold and the Beautiful*, and in the movie *Spy Hard*.

Mike started the 1996 season hitting better than .400 during the first month. "He's the best hitter I ever played with," said long-time centerfielder Brett Butler. But just when it seemed the Dodgers might get to the World Series, they were jolted by a series of setbacks. Third baseman Mike Blowers suffered torn ligaments in his knee and was lost for the year. Brett Butler was diagnosed with throat cancer. (His cancer was treated with radiation therapy.) And worst of all, coach Lasorda suffered a heart attack. He underwent heart surgery June 26. The operation was a success, but a month later he announced his retirement. Mike was heartbroken.

Mike had hit a game-winning homer against the Houston Astros in Lasorda's last game. When Bill Russell took over as manager, Mike gave Russell his first victory by hitting three home runs. At Colorado, Mike homered to center in the fourth and to left in the fifth and eighth innings.

Hall of Fame catcher Johnny Bench, left, met Mike's dad and Mike before a 1993 Los Angeles Dodgers game.

Mike led the Dodgers to the playoffs by hitting .336 with a career-high 36 home runs. Once again, though, Los Angeles was swept in three games, this time by the Braves. When the season ended, Mike went back to Pennsylvania and the cage.

No matter how many times Mike is an All-Star, no matter if the Dodgers win the World Series, no matter what else happens, he will always go back to the cage. He will swing his bat for hours until his hands are covered with blisters and blood. "I'll never take this game for granted, never," Mike says. "I've worked too hard to get here. It's something I've always been taught, and lived by. This game means everything to me, and I'm not about to cheat it. I know this can be gone as easily as it came."

# Career Highlights

## Minor Leagues Statistics

| Year | Level | Team | Games | At bats | Runs | Hits | 2B | 3B | HR | RBIs | BB | Batting average |
|------|-------|------|-------|---------|------|------|-----|-----|-----|------|-----|-----------------|
| 1989 | Rookie | Salem | 57 | 198 | 22 | 53 | 11 | 0 | 8 | 25 | 13 | .268 |
| 1990 | Class A | Vero Beach | 88 | 272 | 27 | 68 | 20 | 0 | 6 | 45 | 11 | .250 |
| 1991 | Class A | Bakersfield | 117 | 448 | 71 | 124 | 27 | 2 | 29 | 80 | 47 | .277 |
| 1992 | Class AA | San Antonio | 31 | 114 | 18 | 43 | 11 | 0 | 7 | 21 | 13 | .377 |
| 1992 | Class AAA | Albuquerque | 94 | 358 | 54 | 122 | 22 | 5 | 16 | 69 | 37 | .341 |
| Totals | | | 387 | 1,390 | 192 | 410 | 91 | 7 | 66 | 240 | 121 | .294 |

2B=doubles, 3B=triples, HR=home runs, BB=bases on balls (walks)

## Honors
• Led California League with .540 slugging percentage.

## Major League Statistics

| Year | Team | Games | At bats | Runs | Hits | 2B | 3B | HR | RBIs | BB | Batting average |
|------|------|-------|---------|------|------|-----|-----|-----|------|-----|-----------------|
| 1992 | Dodgers | 21 | 69 | 5 | 16 | 3 | 0 | 1 | 7 | 4 | .232 |
| 1993 | Dodgers | 149 | 547 | 81 | 174 | 24 | 2 | 35 | 112 | 46 | .318 |
| 1994 | Dodgers | 107 | 405 | 64 | 129 | 18 | 0 | 24 | 92 | 33 | .319 |
| 1995 | Dodgers | 112 | 434 | 82 | 150 | 17 | 0 | 32 | 93 | 39 | .346 |
| 1996 | Dodgers | 148 | 547 | 87 | 184 | 16 | 0 | 36 | 105 | 81 | .336 |
| Totals | | 537 | 2,002 | 319 | 653 | 78 | 2 | 128 | 409 | 203 | .326 |

2B=doubles, 3B=triples, HR=home runs, BB=bases on balls (walks)

## Honors
• National League Rookie of the Year, 1993.
• National League All-Star, 1993, 1994, 1995, 1996.
• Most Valuable Player in the All-Star Game, 1996.

# Glossary

**at bat:** An official attempt to hit a pitched ball. Hitting a sacrifice, being walked, or being hit by a pitch doesn't count as an at bat.

**batting average:** The number of hits a batter gets, divided by the batter's official at bats, carried to three decimal places. For example, if Mike gets 3 hits in 9 at bats, his batting average is .333.

**cleanup spot:** The fourth batting position in the lineup.

**curveball:** A pitch that is thrown so that it spins and moves downward and to the right or left of the batter.

**extra-base hit:** A hit that allows the batter to advance past first base. A *double* gets the batter to second base, a *triple* to third, and a *home run* allows the batter to get all the way back to home plate.

**grand slam:** A home run hit with the bases loaded. A grand slam scores four runs.

**knuckleball:** A slow pitch that is thrown without any spin. The pitch seems to jump around as it approaches the batter.

**on-deck circle:** The area, often outlined in chalk, where the next batter in the order waits.

**opposite field:** Rightfield for a righthanded batter and leftfield for a lefthanded batter.

**pull hitter:** A hitter who hits the ball to leftfield, if righthanded, or rightfield, if lefthanded, because the batter seems to "pull" the ball across his or her body.

**run batted in (RBI):** A run that is scored as a result of a batter getting a hit or, if the bases are loaded, the batter drawing a walk.

**slugging percentage:** The number of bases a batter reaches by hits, divided by the batter's official at bats, carried to three decimal places.

**uppercutting:** Swinging the bat in a big upward arc.

# Index

## Write to Mike:

*You can send mail to Mike at the address on the right. If you write a letter, don't get your hopes up too high. Mike and other athletes get lots of letters every day, and they aren't always able to answer them all.*

Mike Piazza
c/o Los Angeles Dodgers
1000 Elysian Park Avenue
Los Angeles, CA 90012

## Acknowledgements

Photographs are reproduced with the permission of: © ALLSPORT USA/Jed Jacobsohn: p. 1; Reuters/Ray Stubblebine/Archive Photos: pp. 2–3; Reuters/Joe Giza/Archive Photos: p. 6; Los Angeles Dodgers, Inc./Jon Soohoo: pp. 9, 10, 43, 51; © ALLSPORT USA/Al Bello: pp. 13, 14; Barry Taglieber: pp. 16, 19, 23, 30, 34, 38, 44, 52; Seth Poppel Yearbook Archives: p. 26; Archive Photos: p. 33; Miami-Dade Community College, North Campus: p. 37; SportsChrome East/West, Rob Tringali Jr.: p. 48; © John Klein: p. 55; © ALLSPORT USA/ Glenn Cratty: p. 56; Los Angeles Dodgers, Inc./Kevin Miller: p. 59.

Front cover photographs by SportsChrome East/West, Rob Tringali Jr. (left) and © ALLSPORT USA/Otto Greule. Back cover photograph by © Neil Zlozower/Hooked On Drums. Artwork by John Erste.

## About the Author

Jeff Savage is the author of more than 50 books for young readers. A former sportswriter for the San Diego Union-Tribune, Jeff lives with his family in Napa, California.